Depths of Avant-Garde

Sheetal Vadada

BookLeaf Publishing

India | USA | UK

Presentation by *BookLeaf Publishing*

Web: www.bookleafpub.com

E-mail: info@bookleafpub.com

ISBN:9789360941567

First edition 2024

Open

Open to the oceans of emotions
Open to the meadows of magical potions
Open to the puddles of failures and success
Open to oneness and to confess
Open to the nature's essence
Open to the killer quiescence
Open to an open book
Open to the natural look
Open to a different kind of fix
Open to start all over again just like a phoenix!

A
R
H
Q
C
H
Y
U
Z
O
C
R
I
K
F
F
J
B
L
O
S
V
D
U
N
S
I
A
B
M
W
O
F
H
I
K
E
S
M
X

Beauty and Imagination

Sorrow cloud was so depressed, it rained the
whole day in vain…
Snow-blessed mountains frowned as they melted
to drown and turned brown…

The sleek vision of this season went dope with a
reason like a blend of color,
locked in a prison and gray spread all over
without a reason…
Please don't mention that a house without a
pension is a matter of great tension and a mind
without imagination is a life of hallucination!

Reptiles of the marine nation and comics of
caricature don't vibe together and are just a part
of wild creation…
The locality is a widespread center for recreation
where locals drink tea… so like me…
That makes a captured beauty a real lit tea!

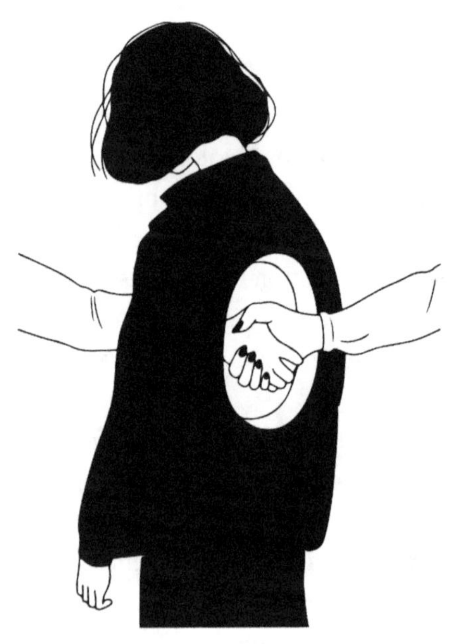

The Seductive Note!

The conductive note turned to a seductive note
when you entered me like a virus through
wireless…

I wanna make it productive without reducting
and your love towards me is so addicting that I
can never be deducting you apart from my
convicting thoughts and writing this my heart is
contracting, acting wired to you with no strings
attached..
Now, none can detach us both!

Well, our kingdom is seldom conducting our
wedding and seducing the virus to us which is
madly multiplexing.
This is a thought-provoking idea that is
convincing and my soul in return receives
through the newly-connected wiring which we
are equally sensing and will frame it with a
picket-fencing!

This is the end of both hearts glancing along
with their emotions dancing!

Dream

You have been a dream!

Magnificent on words
Splendid on deeds
Craving for dreams
Oh! What a greed!

Living for worth
Having thought forth…
What would it cost?
A meal? Deal? Is it a good feel??

Nothing as much as you have been…
None can take the life out of my dream…
Until I have you to be seen.

I will always miss you even in my dream!

Longing

I've been looking for you every day just with a
wish that you'll someday make it to my heart's
gateway!
Always open is my soul's doorway…
Am I going to forget you? No way!

If you are coming, you are no more being let
away…
I will hold you forever and love you in my kind
of way…
This is all I want to say!

I hope you can as well feel things this way…
I would die to see that day...
Awaiting your return… My boo! My dear Bae!

You

I knew it was just you!

I know I am missing you and
I know you are missing me too!
More than this, what else can I do?
Just sit here and imagine you and
find my image in you!

The wind is cold and so are you.
I feel you like winter's dew.
I guess I can sense things without you, barely a
few!

I just loved the window view. Felt like my cup
asked for more coffee to brew!
Everything just sought my attention through.
Oh! What can a night breeze tell me more about
you?

Overall, I forgot to tell you that I love you too!

Worthwhile Days

One Day - Words may be lost.
Another Day - Things done may cost.

Days move fast
Shadows may cast
Leave past things in the past
But from all of it, the long-chosen ones may not
last!

So smile for what you have this while…
As this may vanish with every passing mile!

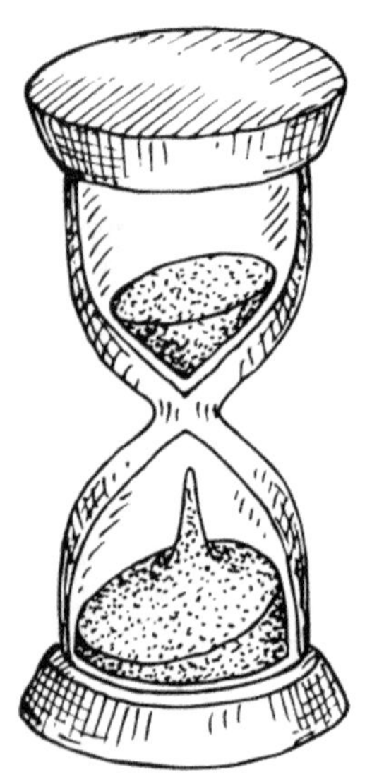

Time ain't Always Great

Time to make and trust to break!
Time to wait and smile to fake
Time to stay awake or live like a happy
heartbreak!
Time is always late to a life's expiry date
Time to win the race to become someone's
bridesmaid!
Time heals all the hate having a tall story to
narrate.
Time could never be great when I wanted time
to recreate
Time to write the destiny of debate with a
low-lying fate because
Time ain't always great!

Women of Steel

It's something about the way you heal…
The way that you feel nobody can deal with this
Woman of Steel.
But I feel that the sand dust dripping from the
cloak of time does a great deal!

Right from begging for a meal to stealing your
zeal from wanting to heal.
Life gears like a rear front reel which would
direct you like an aimless steering wheel.
A roller coaster of emotions that you feel…
Nobody can heal… nobody but you…can deal.

Even your fortune made an appeal
Watching you grow, does an old-fashioned kneel
on my heel!
Wait for it, until you celebrate your suspense
reveal!

Inner Animal

Your inner animal lifts you when you are at your
lowest…
Your inner animal kills the opinions of those
who kill the passion in your life, if you will do
so!
Your inner animal rings your happy bells when
you are high between all the lows...
Your inner animal lives when the soul is dead
and it still glows
Your inner animal impacts when life is on its
dead ends and sea shores
Your inner animal assures you of bringing out
the best in you when with your family and the
worst when with a foe!
Your inner animal is out when you are the very
version of your shadow
Give this inner animal of yours a respectful bow
Who never left you even in the deepest sorrow

Something Less

I wish there were words to describe these
feelings…
I felt something less than happiness…
I felt something less than a craving…
I felt something less than love…
I felt something less than lust…
I felt something less than addiction…
And then, feelings were oblivious of time…
I felt something less than drugs…
I felt something less than lost…
I felt something less than melancholy…
I felt something less than a void…
Now… some things I wish I could avoid.

A Story Untold

Ripe and Tide the words go whirl like hope on
hold…
Ripped untidy, my thoughts go bold like a story
untold…
I wear my heart on my sleeve, a heart of gold…
You have its hold like my old soul got tired and
sold…

Behold! There's another story yet to be told.

She's one of her kind…
Who leaves her mark behind...
Those in the spotlight find her in hindsight…
Irrespective, she decides her way. Never mind!

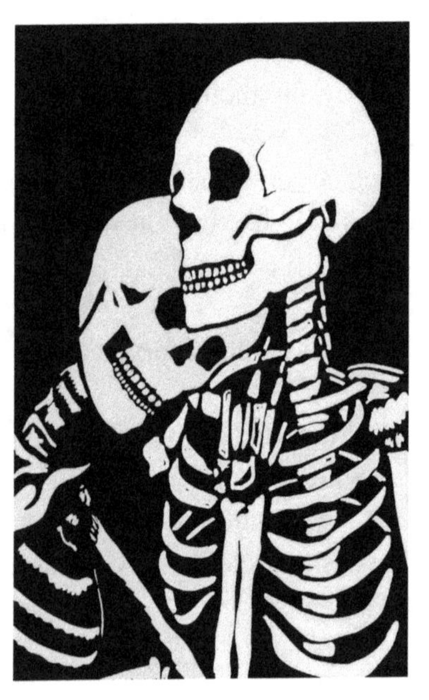

The New Chapter

A comb in my bag…succumb to my lag…
Like a maniac, I hit you right on the track
My love can never get back to the book in my
rack!
Sparkling water… shiny life…
Horror lit up a ghost to whack…
Like a steadfast throwback…
The lucky ones, the diamonds in the sky!

Next Chapter

Messy week— a football to kick!
The story on a brick… vanished with a blink…
Future wives wink at the men in the club…
They've been asked to have a drink
With response motoring the ink
And their cheeks are all pink…
Their love is in sync…
This logic is sick…
Let's put an end to this flick!

But Tattoos Never Die

Everything you think is maybe a lie...
For which I shouldn't have to cry!
But why a goodbye?
Let's think of those days for the last time we had
our high-five!
Nowadays nothing makes up my mood but this
Wi-Fi!
Life is on the low-five
They say some memories never fly
Unless they were secured in heart and not
captured with our naked eye…
Let us give it a new try
Like tattoos that never die.
It can either resemble a purple rain or a dove's
cry!

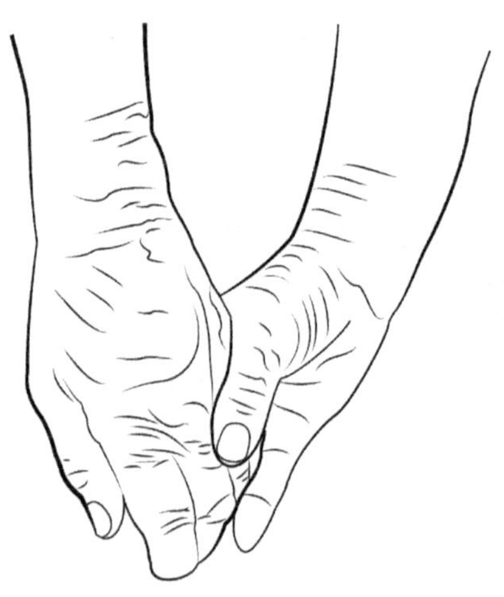

Homage for Old

Soul dead season…
Winter be my reason…
Walking towards a prison.

Stole a stiff stole to wrap my dead soul and be a
bit bold…
But my veins grew old and I was sold to the
homage for old…
The only thing lasting with me was the bronzed
dust and savings of gold stored under an oak
palm tree…

Just like the old soul beside me is shivering with
cold…
Crying her last words… I wish the queen of my
family was a bit beyond bold…
That day, I realized even snow could smoke!
She just dropped dead…Will you hold?

The Wall

It could be so tall that it would hide everything
from them all!
Behind, it could be a green-lush hall
But it only seems beautiful with the dawn's fall
Yet, there is no more reality to it all.
Everything's gone! And now, here stands a big
mall.
This referred to the shrouds of nature's downfall,
It shows the ruptures of the broken wall and the
planet as a hopeless brown ball!
Time passes by and the lush green becomes a
deserted ground call…
This is the story of a past passenger who lately
visited "The Wall"

The Unnatural

It's like a dream come true when those raindrops
touch you and the wind flees you off your feet.

The sky, when you gaze at it, is missing a star's
fleet!
Everything now is to beat the heat and enjoy the
midnight nature's retreat.

Feels like erasing those bad memories and
hitting delete!
To smell the soiled mud and the earth depleted…

With shallow dreams at night buried
In with people, things hurried!

Then those feelings worried.
What if nightmares scurried?

But then, realities would turn out wonderful…
whispered a fairy!

Latex Friendships

Friendships these days are no longer bigger
constructs like shops that never sink… my Stint?
A therapy tint! Pick up a hint?

It's similar to tattoos that ink when you get
sentimental, eyes that wink when you get happy
and calls you fret to share when you are unhappy
so you sit up to drink!

Let that loneliness sink and bring out the lioness
that makes you think…
In this world that's out of latex friendships, is it
ok to just sit there and drink?

Rather sit yourself through with a fruit drink,
dressed up in hot pink, gather yourself on a
skating rink with every fall forgo all the
overthinking—Sadie Sink, play your favorite
music on a radio link…
Let the time sink where the sunlight makes a
gold rink, eyes blink to a vibe check in a party
clink!

Little did I Know

Little did I know, the aroma of how the sandal
was scented and the beautiful walls of the room
were painted.

Little did I know the pain when my car was
dented and my own house had to be rented.

Little did I know the talks turned into memories
when I was devastated and living in a lonely
room because I was frustrated.

Little did I know to see what I needed and to
seek help from the mistreated and whoever felt
defeated

Little did I know the feeling of being enchanted;
I was terrified because those melodies were
always haunted, yet somehow, it felt like I've
always wanted

Little did I know how the written script blended
and was sure to be patented!

A Tree Story

Leaves age unlike the page…

So much rage to mark a bark's gauge…

A tree's stage is untouched until beige…

And then cut down to savage like a reckless old lineage...

A bark with no leaves cried for its salvage

Its transition from the Stone Age to paper turned into garbage..

That is how the life of a cure becomes damaged!

Reminiscence of Love

It is not often that the reminiscence of love is built with lust and fades away with rust

Love can happen over inhuman differences of trust…

But pixies with their fairy dust first created laughter and then lust.

www.ingramcontent.com/pod-product-compliance
Lightning Source LLC
Chambersburg PA
CBHW061728130726
47996CB00006B/2553